TIGER WOODS

By Lucia Raatma

WORLD ALMANAC® LIBRARY

Please visit our web site at: www.worldalmanaclibrary.com
For a free color catalog describing World Almanac® Library's list of high-quality books
and multimedia programs, call 1-800-848-2928 (USA) or 1-800-461-9120 (Canada).
World Almanac® Library's Fax: (414) 332-3567.

Library of Congress Cataloging-in-Publication Data

Raatma, Lucia.
    Tiger Woods / by Lucia Raatma.
       p. cm. — (Trailblazers of the modern world)
    Includes bibliographical references and index.
    Summary: Examines the talents, successful career, and ethnic background of the golfer Tiger Woods.
    ISBN 0-8368-5066-1 (lib. bdg.)
    ISBN 0-8368-5226-5 (softcover)
    1. Woods, Tiger—Juvenile literature. 2. Golfers—United States—Biography—Juvenile literature. 3. Racially
mixed people—United States—Biography—Juvenile literature. [1. Woods, Tiger. 2. Golfers. 3. Racially mixed
people—Biography.] I. Title. II. Series.
    GV964.W66R33   2001
    796.352'092—dc21
    [B]   2001034142

This North American edition first published in 2001 by
World Almanac® Library
330 West Olive Street, Suite 100
Milwaukee, WI 53212 USA

This U.S. edition © 2001 by World Almanac® Library.

An Editorial Directions book
Editor: E. Russell Primm III
Designer and page production: Ox and Company
Photo researcher: Dawn Friedman
Indexer: Timothy Griffin
Proofreader: Neal Durando
World Almanac® Library art direction: Karen Knutson
World Almanac® Library editor: Jacqueline Laks Gorman
World Almanac® Library production: Susan Ashley and Jessica L. Yanke

Photo credits: Corbis/AFP, cover; AllSport USA/Jamie Squire, 4; AllSport USA/J.D. Cuban, 5 top; AP/Wide World
Photos/Charles Rex Arbogast, 5 bottom; Corbis/AFP, 7; AllSport USA/Jamie Squire, 8; Hulton/Archive/John Berry, 9;
Corbis/Alan Levenson, 11; AllSport USA/Ken Levine, 12; AllSport USA/Alan Levenson, 13 top; AP/Wide World Photos,
13 bottom; Hulton/Archive/Orlando Sentinel, 15; Corbis/Don Conrard, 17; AllSport USA/Gary Newkirk, 18;
Hulton/Archive/John Berry, 19 top; AllSport USA/Gary Newkirk, 19 bottom; Hulton/Archive/Cook Online USA, 20;
AP/Wide World Photos/Eric Risberg, 21; AllSport USA/Rusty Garrett, 23; AllSport USA/Patrick Murphy, 24; AP/Wide World
Photos/Phil Sandlin, 26; AP/Wide World Photos/Milwaukee Journal Sentinel, Benny Sieu, 28; AllSport USA/J.D. Cuban, 29;
Hulton/Archive/Reuters/Peter Jones, 30; AllSport USA/J.D. Cuban, 31 top; AllSport USA/David Cannon, 31 bottom; AP/Wide
World Photos/Dave Martin, 32; AP/Wide World Photos/Charles Dharapak, 33 top; Hulton/Archive/Reuters/John Kuntz, 33
bottom; AP/Wide World Photos/George Nikitin, 34; Hulton/Archive/Reuters/Mike Segar, 35 top; AllSport USA/Jamie Squire,
35 bottom; AllSport USA/Craig Jones, 36; AllSport USA/Clive Mason, 37 top; AP/Wide World Photos/Elisa Amendola, 37
bottom; AllSport USA/David Cannon, 38; Hulton/Archive/Reuters/Jeff J. Mitchell, 39; AP/Wide World Photos/Chuck Barton,
40; Hulton/Archive/Joe Raedle, 42; AP/Wide World Photos/Suzanne Plunkett, 43.

Printed in the United States of America

1 2 3 4 5 6 7 8 9 05 04 03 02 01

TABLE of CONTENTS

CHAPTER 1

A WINNING SMILE

Tiger Woods is one of the world's top golfers and a role model for many.

Some people say golf is just a game, nothing to take very seriously. Nevertheless, there are some players who command our attention. They are a pleasure to watch. Golf **clubs** seem to fit so nicely in their hands, and their swing is smooth and easy. Some players seem to have been born to play golf—and Tiger Woods is one of these players.

Tiger is not just another golfer, however. Still in his first years as a professional, he has already helped the game in many ways. Attendance at tournaments has increased, and people are excited about the sport once again. Young people all over the world see Tiger as a role model, and they too want to excel—as golfers as well as in other aspects of their lives.

Tiger has also opened people's eyes to the **racism** that still exists on the golf course, but he has never allowed such **prejudice** to hurt him. His greatest defense against any kind of racism has always been to play his best game. In doing that, he has proved that excellence is a goal for all people, no matter what the color of their skin.

Tiger Woods draws large crowds at golf tournaments.

With his wrist bandaged, Tiger Woods talks to reporters about having to withdraw from a tournament in Southampton, New York.

FACING THE CAMERAS

In the years Tiger Woods has spent on the Professional Golfers Association (PGA) tour, he has had his share of problems with the media. Sometimes, he said the wrong thing, and sometimes he made mistakes that suddenly became headline news. However, through it all, Tiger has maintained his dignity and his honesty, never letting the opinions of others affect his behavior.

BREAKING THE RECORDS

What is remarkable about Tiger Woods's success on the golf course is how dominating he has become in such a short time. Instead of winning a tournament by a single **stroke**, Tiger often sets course records. He's been the youngest winner in the history of some tournaments, and he has broken annual earnings records as well.

However, in spite of all his victories, Tiger has never let his success go to his head. He remains polite and respectful of other players. He plays his heart out, yet he accepts the days when his concentration is off or his swing is not at its best. He is quick to congratulate other players on their wins and compliments them on impressive shots. He is truly a gentleman both on and off the course.

Tiger Woods's face has graced the covers of numerous magazines. He has given thousands of interviews and spoken to hundreds of groups. People all over the world have come to recognize his bright, casual smile. He makes winning look easy sometimes, and he makes the game of golf look like lots of fun.

CHAPTER 2

NEVER TOO YOUNG

Tiger with his mother, Kultida, after winning a tournament in 2000

Tiger Woods was born on December 30, 1975, in Cypress, California. His parents, Earl and Kultida, knew he was special, but no one knew just how extraordinary his life would be. The little boy was nicknamed "Tiger," but his real name was Eldrick. Tiger's mother made up that name, which begins with E for "Earl" and ends with K for "Kultida." She felt that name would make her son feel loved by both parents. He was their only child.

Tiger's nickname came from his father's time as a soldier in Vietnam. Earl had a friend named Colonel Vuong Dang Phong, who was known as "Tiger." The two men were very close, and Earl had fond memories of his friend. Tiger Phong twice saved Earl's life, and for that Earl has remained forever grateful. In honor of their friendship, Earl called his own son "Tiger."

TIGER'S PARENTS

Earl Woods had a long and successful career in the U.S. Army. He was a member of the Green Berets, soldiers who are specially trained for dangerous missions. While Earl was serving in Thailand, he met a woman named Kultida (Tida) Punsawad, whom he liked immediately. Earl had been married before and had three children, but by this time he was divorced. After dating for some time, Earl and Tida decided to marry.

Earl retired from the army and began working for a company that builds planes. He and Tida settled in Cypress, California, a town about 30 miles (48 kilometers) outside Los Angeles. At first, they had a hard time in Cypress. Some of their neighbors objected to their racial background. Earl is part African-American,

Tiger with his father, Earl, on the golf course in 1993

part Chinese, and part Native American. Tida is part Thai, part white, and part Chinese. Before the Woodses moved in, Cypress was an all-white area. People threw garbage at their home, and some even shot at the house with BB guns.

However, Earl and Tida were determined to enjoy their home. They worked in their yard and chatted with their neighbors. Soon the attacks on their house stopped, and the Woodses were accepted for who they are.

EARLY SWINGING

Earl Woods had taken up golf a year or so before Tiger was born. He loved the game, but he wished he had started playing it when he was younger. When Tiger was only a few months old, he liked to watch his father practice. In their garage, Earl practiced hitting golf balls into a net, with Tiger sitting in his high chair, watching his father for hours. Then, one day Tiger started imitating his father. He could barely stand, but he picked up one of the clubs. Tiger could swing it and hit the ball just the way his father did. Earl cheered, and Tiger grinned.

On *The Mike Douglas Show*

When Tiger was only about two years old, people had already started talking about him and his golf skills. He appeared on the local TV news in California and caught the eye of a producer of *The Mike Douglas Show*. Shortly thereafter, Tiger was invited to appear on the program. Tiger wore a red cap along with a red-and-white shirt and khaki shorts. Also on the show that day were Jimmy Stewart, a famous movie star, and Bob Hope, a well-known entertainer who also loves golf.

A little golf green was set up for Tiger and Bob Hope to compete against each another. At one point, Hope joked that they should bet on the next shot, so Tiger moved his ball closer to the hole and tapped it in the **cup**. The audience laughed, and Hope said, "If he doesn't make it as a golfer, he'll make it as a stand-up comic."

As Tiger learned to walk, he continued to practice his golf swing. Before long, his father got him some tiny clubs. Earl was thrilled by his son's skill, and he began taking Tiger with him to play golf. Tiger loved being on the golf course and walking the **fairways** with his dad. Simply put, he loved the game. People couldn't believe that a boy so young could swing a club so well.

A fourteen-year-old Tiger poses with his father and coach.

Tiger loved golf from an early age.

opposite: Young Tiger hitting a golf ball

LOVING THE GAME

It was clear that Tiger loved golf, but his mother made sure he pursued other activities as well. She taught him to read, to write his name, and to do addition and subtraction. She also enjoyed reading books to him. Through it all, Tiger usually carried a golf club with him.

When Tiger was only three years old, he did something amazing—he shot a score of 48 for nine holes at the U.S. Navy Golf Club in Cypress. People who watched that game couldn't believe what they were seeing—this would be a good score for most adults.

Tiger wanted to learn all he could about golf. He knew there were usually eighteen holes to shoot, and he knew about the different kinds of clubs. However, his father realized he had to teach him more, so Earl began to teach Tiger about concentrating. He wanted Tiger to do the same things each time he got ready to hit a ball, so he taught Tiger a routine: getting behind the ball, looking at the target, and then judging the wind and distance. It was hard at first, but Tiger learned well. Indeed, he would call upon the patience and concentration he mastered as a child while playing important tournaments in his future.

THE FIRST COMPETITION

When Tiger was four, Earl thought he was ready to play in junior tournaments, but most of those were for golfers at least ten years old. There was one tournament, however, in which Tiger was allowed to play. This competition was for three different kinds of shots: **driving**, **pitching**, and **putting**. Driving means hitting the ball in the air for a long distance. Pitching means hitting the ball in the air for a short distance. Putting means hitting the ball on the **green**, usually for a short distance.

The other kids in the tournament were six and seven years older than Tiger, but he didn't let that bother him. He remembered what his father had taught him and concentrated on every shot. His hard work paid off, and he came in second! In the years to come, there would be many more competitions. Tiger was off to a good start.

Jack Nicklaus, the Golden Bear

Jack Nicklaus began playing golf when he was ten years old and, in his late teens, he was considered one of the greatest amateur golfers ever to play the game. In his first year as a professional, Nicklaus won the U.S. Open golf tournament. He then went on to win the other three tournaments in golf's **Grand Slam**—the Masters (six times), the British Open (three times), and the PGA Championship (five times). And he won the U.S. Open three more times as well. Many feel he is the greatest golfer ever.

Nicklaus, who is nicknamed the "Golden Bear," designs golf courses as well as playing golf. As a little boy, Tiger looked up to Nicklaus and hoped one day to be much like him. Over the years, many people have compared Tiger to Nicklaus, and there are some who feel Tiger will break all the Golden Bear's records.

CHAPTER 3

AT SCHOOL AND ON THE COURSE

When Tiger started school, his mother's efforts at home really showed. He was eager to learn and was a very bright student. Even as a young child, he was alert and ready, preparing for his classes and always trying hard.

AN INTRODUCTION TO RACISM

On Tiger's first day of kindergarten, he had a difficult experience, however. A group of white sixth-graders did not like the idea of Tiger attending their school. They ganged up on him, beat him up, and tied him to a tree. They wrote a racist word on his shirt, and they called him names and threw rocks at him.

Tiger did not understand why he was being treated that way. He didn't know the other boys, and he had done nothing to hurt them. Unfortunately, the boys chose to dislike Tiger just because of his skin color. They didn't take the time to get to know him. Over the years, Tiger has experienced racism in many ways, but he has learned to stand up to prejudice, in both his personal and professional life, and focus on his own goals.

In the years to come, Tiger and his father were often denied the right to play at certain golf courses. Golf had long been a game for white men, and for decades many country clubs would not allow people of color (or, for some time, women of any race) to use their facilities. However, Tiger Woods was able to fight this racism by playing golf at a new level of excellence. His success has helped open the game to people of all backgrounds.

SPECIAL RULES

Tiger's parents were proud of his success on the golf course, but they agreed that school must come first. Tiger was expected to finish all his homework before he played golf.

Tiger was also expected to be polite. He was taught to respect other people and have good manners. His parents trusted him to behave well no matter where he was—at home, at school, or on the golf course. Very often, sports figures lose their temper when they play. Tennis stars throw their racquets, football stars fight with other players, and basketball stars argue with the referee. Tiger understood at a very young age that he was not to behave in this way. His mother often said, "You'll be a gentleman when you play. I'll have no one saying I raised a spoiled child."

MORE TOURNAMENTS

When Tiger was eight years old, he entered the Optimist International Junior World tournament. As usual, the other players were all older than he was. His parents told him to have fun and not to worry about the competition, but Tiger took the contest very seriously.

Tiger has always been a well-mannered golfer who focuses on the game.

An Important Influence

As an adult, Tiger has acknowledged the role his parents played in making him who he is. In the introduction to *Playing Through*, a book by Earl Woods, Tiger wrote the following:

So much of who I am comes from my parents. Although I am an only child, my mother and father never spoiled me. I am the product of their careful guidance and discipline, which hopefully helps bring out the best in me. The many ideals and lessons I've learned from my mother and father define who I am and make me proud of who I am. Their unwavering trust and confidence in me keep me going each day.

He concentrated, just as he had been taught. He took his time at the **tee**, and his drives were long and well placed. He putted with incredible focus. People were amazed as they watched this young boy move along the course. No one had expected him to win, but he did. And over the years, he won the same championship three more times.

When he was thirteen years old, Tiger entered the Insurance Youth Classic. This tournament—called the Big I—pairs amateur players with professionals. In his first attempt, Tiger came in second, and the next year, he placed first. At fourteen, he was the youngest winner ever.

In addition to these successes, Tiger entered and won dozens of other tournaments. People were starting to know his name well, and other young players saw him as the person to beat. Some were even calling him the next Jack Nicklaus.

HAVING FUN

Tiger's parents wanted him to have a happy childhood, and they encouraged him to have fun. He enjoyed rap music and video games just like other kids, but he assured his father and mother that the most fun he could have was by playing golf. He tried other sports, including football, baseball, and track, but he always came back to golf. He once told his dad, "That's how I enjoy myself, by shooting low scores."

A Religion of Respect

Tiger's mother is a Buddhist, and she shared her beliefs with her son. One Buddhist principle is taking responsibility for one's actions, so Tiger learned never to blame anyone else for his mistakes. Another important Buddhist idea is respect. Tiger was taught to be kind to all people, no matter what their background. Buddhists also believe in hard work. Over the years, Tiger has appreciated the ideas his mother instilled in him, and he has often relied on these beliefs in his personal life as well as in his golf game.

MAKING A NAME FOR HIMSELF

In 1991, Tiger entered the U.S. Junior Amateur Championship. At fifteen, he believed he could win the tournament even though he'd be up against the best young golfers in the United States.

The tournament was held in Orlando, Florida, and the weather that July was hot. As the players reached the final round, Tiger began to feel the pressure to win. He made some mistakes and was soon three shots behind the leader, Brad Zwetschke. At that point, Tiger remembered all that his father had taught him. He concentrated on his shots and tried not to think about what the other players were doing.

His strategy paid off. As they reached the last hole, Tiger and Brad were tied. However, Tiger kept his mind on the game, while Brad seemed to get nervous. When it was over, Tiger had won by a single stroke!

Tiger became the youngest player ever to win that tournament. He was named *Golf Digest* Player of the Year, Titleist-*Golfweek* Amateur of the Year, and Southern California Player of the Year. He was proud of all he had accomplished and eager to see what the future would hold.

CHAPTER 4

THINKING ABOUT THE FUTURE

In 1992, Tiger played in the Nissan Open in Los Angeles.

In 1992, Tiger Woods won the U.S. Junior Amateur Championship a second time, and he won it again the following year. There seemed to be no stopping the young golfer. However, his life was not without its challenges.

PLAYING WITH THE PROS

When he was a sophomore in high school, Tiger received a very special invitation. He was asked to play in the Nissan Open, a tournament for professional players. Since it was held in Los Angeles, close to his California home, he was easily able to attend.

Playing with professional golfers was very exciting for Tiger, and he knew it was a great honor. Unfortunately, he did not play his best game. Maybe the noise of the crowds got to him, or maybe he was a little nervous about being there. In any case, Tiger tried to make the best of the experience. He said, "I learned I'm not that good. I've got a lot of growing to do." That honesty and maturity helped Tiger improve his skills.

Golf has taught Tiger, here with two young fans, a lot about life.

Things haven't always gone smoothly for Tiger on the golf course.

ANOTHER DISAPPOINTMENT

Soon after winning the U.S. Junior Amateur Championship for the third time, Tiger entered the U.S. Amateur tournament. This was the next step for him, and some felt he was favored to win. It would have been great to win both tournaments in the same year, but it wasn't meant to be.

Tiger began the tournament well, but soon his drives were off, and he was not hitting the ball solidly. He fell behind and then also had to wait out a five-hour thunderstorm. In the end, Paul Page won the tournament. Tiger tried to understand what he had done wrong, and he set himself the goal to win the next year.

Tiger, second from left, and his high school varsity golf team

THINKING ABOUT COLLEGE

As Tiger began his senior year in high school, many colleges were interested in him, since they knew he would be a great asset to their golf teams. Arizona and Arizona State contacted him, as did the University of Virginia, Stanford University, and the University of Nevada at Las Vegas (UNLV). Tiger's parents decided that Tiger should choose what college he would attend. They let him talk to the various coaches and visit the campuses.

Earl and Tida believed that their son was old enough to make this decision on his own. They were impressed with the questions Tiger asked when he visited the schools, and they appreciated the amount of research he put into the choice. Tiger was most impressed by the golf program at UNLV, and the sunny weather there appealed to him too. However, in the end he chose Stanford because it has a strong academic reputation, which was very important to him.

Wally Goodwin, the golf coach at Stanford, was thrilled with Tiger's decision. He had been watching the young man's progress on the golf course, and he knew Tiger would be an important member of the Stanford team.

Father and Son

Tiger and Earl Woods share a very special relationship. They are close in a way that some parents and children are not. In fact, they feel they can talk to each other about anything. Earl explains, "Tiger and I maintained a central line of communication, always based on openness, caring, and plenty of emotion." Earl always told his son to question things, to look for answers on his own, and Tiger has done that. Earl remembers, "Tiger began questioning me more, too, and I encouraged that. I'm always willing to admit my mistakes and I freely admit them to my son. . . ."

Over the years, Earl has had some health problems, which sometimes keep him from being at the course when his son plays. However, Tiger always knows that his father is there with him, even if he is only watching him on television or keeping him in his thoughts. As Tiger says, "Pop wears many hats in our relationship. He is my counselor, my coach, my conscience, my inspiration, and my hero."

TEAM TIGER

By that time, Earl Woods knew how special his son was, and he knew it was his responsibility to surround Tiger with talented, supportive people. Among the members of "Team Tiger" are Butch Harmon, Tiger's swing coach, and Jay Brunza, his sports psychologist. Many athletes, both young and old, work with psychologists so they can learn to handle the pressures of winning and the challenges of losing. Jay has played a key role in helping Tiger remain focused both on and off the golf course.

THE U.S. AMATEUR CHAMPIONSHIP

Before he entered college, Tiger had one thing he wanted to accomplish. He wanted to win the U.S. Amateur title he had lost the year before. So in August 1994, he joined the other players at Sawgrass Country Club in Ponte Vedra, Florida. He did well in the early rounds, and by the final day of the tournament he was in contention for the title. The amateur tournaments are set up as **match play**, so Tiger was paired with Trip Kuehne for the last thirty-six holes.

Jay Brunza, Tiger's sports psychologist, served as his **caddy** for the tournament. Jay tried to keep Tiger relaxed yet focused, but after thirteen holes, Tiger was down by six shots. The weather was hot and humid, and Tiger was having trouble concentrating. He attempted to remember all that his father had taught him, and he tried to forget about the crowd of people watching. Instead, he just thought about the ball and getting it into the cup. Slowly, his concentration improved.

After twenty-seven holes, Tiger moved within three strokes of Trip Kuehne. After the thirty-fourth hole, the two players were tied. Then, on the next hole, Tiger made a difficult shot, which resulted in a **birdie**. He held on to the lead and won the championship. He pumped his arm in victory—a gesture he has often used since. Tiger was the youngest person ever to win the U.S. Amateur Championship. The next year, he became the first person to win the title twice.

AS A STANFORD STUDENT

When Tiger went off to college, Earl and Tida knew that their lives would never be the same. They were sad to see him go, but they were excited for him too. Earl realized that his son was "traveling a road that . . . was going to take him places no one had ever been." He knew that his son's future was bright.

In 1994, Tiger became the youngest winner of the U.S. Amateur Championship.

At Stanford, Tiger had to do all the things other freshmen have to do. He carried golf bags for the older players on the team and lived in a dormitory. He was energized by the atmosphere at college. He met people who were smarter than he was, and he took classes that were difficult and challenging.

Nevertheless, Tiger also had some hard times. On one occasion, he was robbed at knifepoint. At other times, he got threatening phone calls and letters, usually racist in content. Some people did not feel that Tiger deserved all the attention he was getting. Tiger did not understand the hatred some people could have for him, especially people he had never even met.

During his first year at Stanford, Tiger did well both in class and on the course, but sometimes it was hard to juggle studying, practicing, and traveling to tournaments. However, Tiger tried to do his best as a student and as a golfer. He spent long hours practicing and devoted time to improving his driving and putting. Over the years, Tiger would become known for his remarkable strength and beautiful drives.

Since Tiger was the U.S. Amateur champion, he was invited to play in the four Grand Slam tournaments—the Masters, the U.S. Open, the British Open, and the PGA (Professional Golfers Association) Championship. Participating was exciting for Tiger, but it was also exhausting. The Masters is held

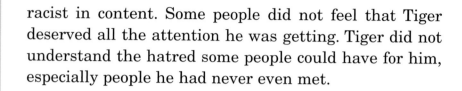

At Stanford University, Tiger was an asset to the golf team.

The Question of Race

At one point early in his career, Tiger Woods decided it was time to talk to the media about his racial heritage. Here is part of what he had to say:

My parents have taught me to always be proud of my ethnic background. Please rest assured that is, and always will be, the case—past, present, and future. The media has portrayed me as African-American; sometimes, Asian. In fact, I am both.

Yes, I am the product of two great cultures—one African-American and the other Asian.

On my father's side, I am African-American. On my mother's side, I am Thai. Truthfully, I feel very fortunate, and EQUALLY PROUD, to be both African-American and Asian!

The critical and fundamental point is that ethnic background and/or composition should NOT make a difference. It does NOT make a difference to me. The bottom line is that I am an American . . . and proud of it!

That is who I am and what I am. Now, with your cooperation, I hope I can just be a golfer and a human being.

in the spring, so Tiger had to play and then return to college in time for final exams. He did not finish well in these tournaments on his first tries, but he looked forward to playing in them in the years to come.

Tiger's efforts were noted as he was named *Golf World*'s Man of the Year and honored as the *Los Angeles Times* Player of the Year. And in 1995, he was named First Team All-American.

In spite of this success, Tiger was having trouble with the National Collegiate Athletic Association (NCAA), which has specific rules about what college athletes can and cannot do. Often these rules seemed unreasonable to Tiger. For instance, a local country club wanted to give Tiger membership privileges, but the NCAA ruled that he could not accept. Also, the NCAA suspended Tiger for playing the Masters with golf clubs that the Stanford team did not use.

The NCAA was also upset after Tiger had dinner with golf great Arnold Palmer. Tiger considered Palmer to be a friend, and he saw the dinner as a great opportunity to talk about golf with a professional player. Palmer had invited Tiger and so he paid the bill. Tiger had enjoyed the evening, but the NCAA ruled that the

As amateur champion, Tiger Woods made friends with golf greats Arnold Palmer, left, and Jack Nicklaus, center.

A Love of Practice

All good athletes have to put in hours and hours of practice, and Tiger Woods is no exception. Earl Woods explained it this way:

The first thing I taught Tiger, aside from the love of the game of golf, was the love of practice. That prevails in him today— the sheer joy of practicing, of having fun while practicing. I taught him that there are no shortcuts. Nobody owes you anything. The game doesn't owe you anything. You get out of it what you put into it.

dinner was inappropriate and talked of suspending Tiger from playing golf. The media carried the story all over the country. In the end, Tiger was not suspended, but Earl Woods was convinced that the NCAA was trying to make life difficult for his son.

After two years at Stanford, Tiger began to wonder about all the NCAA rules. Much as he loved college, he hated being watched. He began to think more about his future.

CHAPTER 5

ON THE PGA TOUR

Clasping his father's hand, Tiger announces his decision to turn professional.

As the summer of 1996 came to an end, Tiger decided not to return to Stanford University. Many people had been wondering when the young man was going to turn pro. That August, Tiger decided it was time. Earlier in the year, he had won the NCAA individual title, and over the summer he had won his third U.S. Amateur Championship. After that success, he knew there was little left for him to accomplish as an amateur, so he held a press conference and told the world his decision.

WITHIN THE PGA

Many people supported Tiger's decision to turn professional, but some of his fellow golfers thought he wasn't ready. They made negative comments about Tiger's age and his ability. To those people, Earl Woods was quick to say, "He's ready to take on anyone. Maybe some of these guys are just a little bit scared of the new guy on the block."

In his first tournament as a professional, Tiger tied for sixtieth place. In his second appearance, he came in eleventh, and in his next tournament, he placed fifth.

Tiger playing professional golf in Milwaukee

Then in his fourth appearance, he came in third. Tiger clearly was improving his game and coming to understand the pressures of being a professional player, but those several weeks had been exhausting.

His next tournament was to be the Buick Challenge in Pine Mountain, Georgia. Even though he was a young player and still without a win, Tiger drew crowds and tournament directors were eager to book him. So the Buick Challenge organizers were furious when Tiger suddenly pulled out of their competition. Tiger didn't intend to offend anyone. He was just tired and needed a break, but the people at the Buick Challenge did not understand. They called him "ungrateful" and asked for an official apology.

Tiger couldn't believe the reaction. He quickly wrote letters of apology to everyone involved. He admitted that, at age twenty, he had made a mistake. After a few weeks, the tournament organizers seemed to forgive that mistake, and Tiger prepared for his next competition.

ROOKIE OF THE YEAR

Supported by his caddy, Mike "Fluff" Cowan, and his swing coach, Butch Harmon, Tiger arrived at the Las Vegas Invitational ready to play. On his first day, he shot a 70—not the score he was hoping for—but the second day, he shot a 63. (**Par**, an average score, on this course was 72; most courses have pars of 70, 71, or 72. Professional players always hope to shoot scores below par.) By the last day of the tournament, Tiger was tied with Davis Love III. Tiger remained focused and assured. He talked with Fluff and took his time between shots. In the end, he won by a single stroke. It was only his fifth tournament as a pro, and it was his first win!

Caddie Mike "Fluff" Cowan gives Tiger some advice.

Soon after, Tiger placed third in the LaCantera Texas Open. Then he played in the Disney Classic in Orlando, Florida, and posted his second PGA win. By the end of 1996, Tiger was ranked thirty-third in the world. The PGA named him Rookie of the Year and *Sports Illustrated* honored him as Sportsman of the Year.

Tiger holding up his first professional trophy

below: Fans at the 1997 Masters Tournaments in Atlanta, Georgia, watch Tiger play.

ON TO AUGUSTA

In the spring of 1997, Tiger Woods traveled to Augusta, Georgia, for the Masters Tournament. He wanted to win his first Grand Slam title, but some people still thought he wasn't ready. Tiger was confident, though, and he knew he could do it if he played his best.

On the first day of the four-day tournament, he shot a 70. He was not pleased with the effort and knew he could do better. On the second day, he shot a 66 and sat in first place. The next day, he shot a 65. This score was seven under par and it put him nine strokes ahead of the player in second place.

On the final day of the Masters, Tiger was ready to make history. He birdied the second hole, but then he shot a **bogey** on the fifth and the

The Tiger Woods Era

Writing about Tiger's first PGA win, Gary Van Sickle of *Sports Illustrated* explained the impact the young man was having on the game:

Golf, as we know it, is over. It came to an end on a . . . Sunday evening in Las Vegas when Tiger Woods went for the upgrade: He's not just a promising young Tour pro anymore, he's an era.

A History of the Masters

In 1934, Bob Jones and Clifford Roberts began the tournament in Augusta, Georgia. At first it was known as the Augusta National Invitation Tournament. Five years later, it was renamed the Masters Tournament, and since then, many masters of golf have participated in this four-day event. Past winners include Ben Hogan, Arnold Palmer, and Seve Ballesteros. Jack Nicklaus won the tournament six times.

Winners of the Masters are given a green jacket that has come to symbolize the tournament. When Tiger Woods won the Masters, 1996 champion Nick Faldo held the green jacket out for Tiger to wear. He became the first player of color to win this prestigious title.

seventh. He knew it was time to concentrate. On the next hole, he shot a birdie. Then he birdied a few more holes, and there seemed no stopping him. Tiger not only won the Masters that year, but he won by twelve strokes—eighteen under par! His final score set a Masters record, and he was also the youngest person ever to win the tournament. Cameras flashed as Tiger walked off the eighteenth green and embraced his parents. It was a special day for him—and for the world of golf.

Tiger celebrates with his mother after winning the 1997 Asian Honda Classic in Thailand.

FINISHING HIS FIRST YEAR AS A PRO

Later in 1997, Tiger Woods won the Asian Honda Classic in Thailand, and he was especially proud of this victory in his mother's native country. He also won a number of other PGA events and was named PGA Player of the Year. He became the youngest player (at twenty-one years and twenty-four weeks) to be ranked number one in the world.

Lee Elder

Lee Elder was born in July 1934, the year the Masters Tournament came into being. However, for much of Elder's life, golf was not open to black players. In fact, black players were not allowed to play at most private golf clubs in the United States. In 1975, Elder made history by becoming the first man of color to play in the Masters Tournament. He played there again in 1977 and was a member of the 1979 U.S. Ryder Cup team, the group of players from the United States who competes each year against a European team.

Lee Elder was at the Masters in 1997 and had come to watch Tiger Woods make history. Before the final round, he said to Tiger, "You do it, son." Tiger indeed did it, and Tiger recognized what Lee Elder had done for him and for the sport of golf.

CHAPTER 6

GOLF AND BEYOND

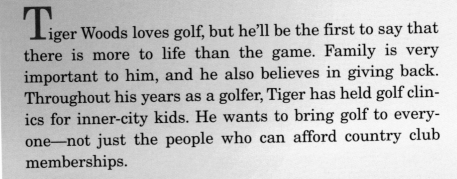

Tiger Woods loves golf, but he'll be the first to say that there is more to life than the game. Family is very important to him, and he also believes in giving back. Throughout his years as a golfer, Tiger has held golf clinics for inner-city kids. He wants to bring golf to everyone—not just the people who can afford country club memberships.

Tiger gives some golf tips to a young golfer at a 1999 clinic in San Francisco.

THE TIGER WOODS FOUNDATION

At the 1997 Phoenix Open, Tiger announced the creation of the Tiger Woods Foundation. The purpose of this project is to use golf as a way to reach children and their families. The

Big Dreams

Once while addressing a youth group, Tiger Woods explained his philosophy:

There are no shortcuts in golf, and there are no shortcuts in life. You have to work for it. Dream big and keep your dreams for yourself. Because the dreams that you have are those things that separate you from others. If you give up your dream, you give up hope. And without hope, you are nothing.

foundation urges parents to be involved with their children, and it also teaches responsibility to young people. Tiger hopes that by playing golf, children will learn about themselves and gain confidence.

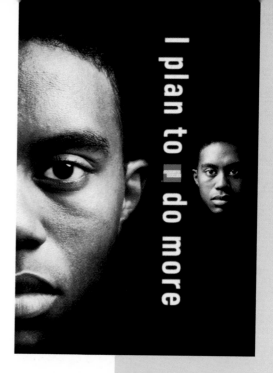

I plan to do more

LIVING UP TO EXPECTATIONS

In the months after the 1997 Masters, much was expected of Tiger Woods. Reporters wanted interviews, and companies wanted him as their spokesperson. Tiger had been in the spotlight before, but this was different. He tried to just enjoy his time at his Orlando home. He tried to focus on golf and have fun away from the course, but Tiger seldom felt as though he had any time for himself. During this period, he began changing his swing. He knew that he could play better golf, and he decided it was important to make this adjustment. However, perfecting his swing took time, and some people wondered when he would enjoy another PGA win.

In 1997, Tiger Woods appeared in American Express advertisements.

Tiger working on his game with swing coach, Butch Harmon

People had talked of his winning all four Grand Slam tournaments in 1997, but this was not a fair expectation. He didn't win the other three majors, and he struggled in his playing. For the next several months, Tiger experienced a slight slump. His swing was still not right, and his putting was below standard. It was a difficult time for him because he had tasted success and wanted more. To his credit, Tiger got help. He turned to his father and Butch Harmon for advice. He also spent time with Jay Brunza, working on his game and on his mind.

In February 1999, Tiger won the Buick Invitational in San Diego, California. He was pleased about the win, and he felt his game was improving. The next month, he made another change when he and caddy Fluff Cowan decided to part ways. Tiger replaced him with Steve Williams, a New Zealander who has been caddying since he was fifteen. Tiger commented about Steve, "He's so positive out there, keeps me upbeat." For his part, Steve was pleased with the opportunity to work with Tiger, a player whom he calls "the perfect partner."

Later that year, when he arrived in Medinah, Illinois, for the 1999 PGA Championship, Tiger approached the tournament as he would any other, but the event turned out to be a special one. By the final day, Tiger was in the lead, yet he was closely trailed by Sergio Garcia, a hot young player. Sergio had made it

Tiger talks to Sergio Garcia at the 1999 PGA Championship in Medinah, Illinois.

known that he wanted to win, but of course Tiger had other ideas.

Sergio has great energy on the golf course, and the crowd loved him. Tiger tried to block out the crowd and just kept playing the best golf he could. He struggled with a few bogeys, and he knew that Sergio was playing well. In the end, Tiger won the tournament by a single stroke. At long last, Tiger had won his second Grand Slam title.

Also in 1999, Tiger teamed with Mark O'Meara, a friend and fellow golfer, in the World Cup competition, an international tournament of individual players and two-man teams. Tiger won the individual title, while he and Mark brought home the team title. In addition, he won eight PGA tournaments. As the year ended, Tiger had much to be happy about.

Tiger with fellow golfer Mark O'Meara in 1999

The Nike Commercials

When Tiger turned pro in 1996, Nike was already eager to sign him. By the time Tiger played in his very first professional tournament, people could count sixteen Nike logos on his clothing. Other companies—including Titleist, Buick, and Wheaties—have used Tiger in advertising as well, but Nike is probably the best known.

In his Nike commercials, Tiger has appealed to a very wide audience. He has performed trick golf shots, and he has provided inspiration for other players. The Nike contract has been very profitable for Tiger. In fact, some say Tiger was a millionaire before he hit his first ball as a professional.

CHAPTER 7

A REMARKABLE RUN

Tiger Woods played in the 100th U.S. Open in Pebble Beach, California.

The twenty-four-year-old Tiger Woods did amazing things in the years 2000 and 2001. He didn't just win tournaments, he won major tournaments, and he won them big.

THE U.S. OPEN

Beautiful Pebble Beach, California, was the setting for the 2000 U.S. Open, and all eyes were on Tiger. He had come in only fifth at the 2000 Masters, but as Butch Harmon explained, "Tiger came here with one thing in mind: to win this tournament."

Tiger opened with a 65 for the first round. On the second day of play, he was paired with his boyhood hero, Jack Nicklaus. The two walked from hole to hole together and showed each other the greatest respect. At the end of the day, Nicklaus didn't make the cut, so he did not participate in the final two days of play. Surely he was disappointed, but he seemed to be happy about passing the torch to Tiger.

By the end of the final round, Tiger had built a fifteen-stroke lead. He won the tournament with a twelve-under-par score, setting a U.S.

Open record. Even Nicklaus himself admitted, "There isn't a flaw in his game or his makeup. He will win more majors than Arnold Palmer and me combined. Somebody is going to dust my records. It might as well be Tiger, because he's such a great kid."

THE BRITISH OPEN

A month after the U.S. Open victory, Tiger traveled to St. Andrews, Scotland, to play in the British Open. The other golfers knew that Tiger was the man to beat, but no one was successful in that effort.

At the end of the tournament, Tiger had won again, this time with an eight-stroke margin. This win made him only the fifth person in history—and the youngest—to win all four Grand Slam titles. The other men on that list are the legendary golfers Gene Sarazen, Ben Hogan, Gary Player, and Jack Nicklaus.

THE PGA CHAMPIONSHIP

Valhalla in Louisville, Kentucky, hosted the PGA Championship in August 2000. Tiger was having a good year and hoped to score another victory, but golf veteran Bob May wanted to prevent him from doing so. At the end of the final round, Tiger and Bob were tied.

Silencing the Critics

After Tiger Woods won the 2000 U.S. Open, Clifton Brown of *The New York Times* had this to say:

There was a time, when Woods first turned professional, when people wondered if he had the game to win an Open, whether he had enough accuracy off the tee, or enough control with his short irons, or enough patience. Those questions have been silenced. Woods can win on any golf course that has tee boxes, fairways, and greens.

The winner of the 2000 British Open kisses his trophy.

The two men had to play three additional holes of golf to break the tie. These playoffs can be very tense, since any mistake can mean the difference between a loss and a win. In the end, Tiger prevailed, winning by just one stroke. With that title, Tiger became one of the few players to win three Grand Slam championships in a single year.

Tiger shakes hands with Jack Nicklaus after finishing a round of play.

ENDING THE YEAR

Tiger went on the win the 2000 Canadian Open in addition to the Memorial Tournament, the Mercedes Championship, and others. Clearly, he was dominating the sport of golf, and there was little anyone could do to stop him. About his game, Tiger said, "I'm going to try to get better. I'm not going to win every tournament I play in, but I'm going to try."

2001 AND THE TIGER SLAM

As 2001 began, some people began to say Tiger Woods was in a slump. He went for a few months without winning a PGA tournament, leading certain reporters to speculate that perhaps he was not as dominant as once thought. However, he broke that so-called slump in March by winning the Bay Hill Invitational and then winning the very next tournament, the Players Championship. Those two victories made him the frontrunner for the 2001 Masters.

When he arrived in Augusta, Georgia, in April 2001, reporters, spectators, and fellow golfers wondered if Tiger could do it again. Could he win his second Masters and thereby win the four major PGA titles in a row? The term Grand Slam had been invented many years before to describe winning all four major titles in one year. Before Tiger, no one had accomplished that feat, and no one had come close to winning all four in a row. Some said that by winning the Masters, Tiger would not achieve a Grand Slam, since he wouldn't have won all the titles in one calendar year. Others said that winning all four in a row would be enough.

On the final day of play, Tiger Woods put on a remarkable performance. He, David Duval, and Phil Mickelson all had a chance at the title, but in the end, Tiger prevailed. He won the Masters and suddenly was the title-holder of all four major championships—the 2000 U.S. Open, 2000 British Open, 2000 PGA, and 2001 Masters—a historic feat. Immediately, the debate began. Was it a Grand Slam or not? Some in the media gave the

Breaking the Records

Here are just some of the records Tiger Woods has set so far:

1991	Became the youngest player ever to win the U.S. Junior Amateur Championship
1994	Became the youngest player ever to win the U.S. Amateur Championship
1996	Reached $1 million in earnings after only nine events
1997	Set PGA record with five wins in the first sixteen tournaments
1997	Won Masters Tournament with twelve-stroke victory and eighteen-under-par score
1999	Won $6,615,585—more money than any other golfer in a single year
2000	Won U.S. Open by fifteen strokes
2000	Became the youngest player to win all four Grand Slam tournaments
2001	Became the only player ever to win all four Grand Slam tournaments consecutively

The Goals of the Foundation

Tiger Woods is dedicated to the work of his foundation. He says:

I am more proud of my involvement with the Tiger Woods Foundation than any tournament I've ever won. Through the game of golf, we're able to spread the good word about sportsmanship, family relationships, education, and solid values—building blocks that will make our world a better place.

achievement the perfect name: a Tiger Slam. No matter what it was called, everyone agreed that Tiger Woods had managed to do something truly amazing, not just in golf but in the entire world of sports.

MORE TO COME

As Tiger Woods reaches his mid-twenties, there is no doubt that he has much to look forward to. There will probably be many more tournament wins for him, and surely he will continue to be a celebrity throughout the world. However, such success does not mean that Tiger will get lazy. He continues to run many miles a week, as well as lifting weights and working out on a regular basis. Tiger knows that he has to be a good all-around athlete in order to win.

Aside from winning, Tiger has many other goals. One is to make golf open to all people, no matter what their background. Another is to reach kids and help them be the best they can be. Through work with his foundation, he hopes to achieve these goals.

opposite: Inspired by Tiger Woods, kids from a variety of ethic backgrounds have started playing golf.

Tiger Woods accepts an award from *Sports Illustrated* for outstanding achievement.

TIMELINE

1975 Is born on December 30 in Cypress, California

1978 Appears on *The Mike Douglas Show*

1979 Shoots a 48 for nine holes at the U.S. Navy Golf Club

1984 Wins Optimist International Junior World title; repeats in 1985, 1988, and 1989

1991 Wins the U.S. Junior Amateur Championship; repeats in 1992 and 1993

1994 Wins U.S. Amateur Championship; repeats in 1995 and 1996; enters Stanford University

1996 Wins NCAA Championship; turns pro; wins Las Vegas Invitational, his first PGA victory; named PGA Rookie of the Year

1997 Wins Masters Tournament; is ranked number one in the world; named PGA Player of the Year; establishes the Tiger Woods Foundation

1999 Wins PGA Championship; participates in U.S. Ryder Cup Team win over Europe; named PGA Player of the Year

2000 Wins U.S. Open Championship, British Open, PGA Championship, and Canadian Open

2001 Wins Masters Tournament; becomes the first to hold all four Grand Slam titles simultaneously

GLOSSARY

birdie: one stroke under par on a hole

bogey: one stroke over par on a hole

caddy: the person who carries a golfer's bag, hands the golfer clubs and balls, and provides advice and support

clubs: the tools a golfer uses to hit balls—woods, irons, and putters

cup: the hole into which a golfer hits a ball

driving: hitting the ball a long distance, especially as the first shot on a given hole

fairways: the large grassy areas between the tees and the greens

Grand Slam: the four major tournaments in the PGA tour: the Masters, the U.S. Open, the British Open, and the PGA Championship; to win a Grand Slam is to win all four titles in one year

green: the smooth grassy area surrounding a hole

match play: competition between two golfers or two teams of golfers

par: the standard number of strokes that a golfer should need to reach a particular hole

pitching: hitting a golf ball in the air, usually for a short distance

prejudice: unequal treatment or denial of rights

putting: hitting the ball on a golf green, usually for a short distance

racism: unequal treatment based on a person's race

stroke: the swing of a golf club in order to hit the ball

tee: a wooden peg that holds the golf ball in position for the first shot of each hole

TO FIND OUT MORE

BOOKS

Christopher, Matt. *On the Course with . . . Tiger Woods.* Boston: Little, Brown, 1998.

Durbin, William. *Tiger Woods: Golf Legends.* Broomall, Penn.: Chelsea House, 1998.

Edwards, Nicholas. *Tiger Woods: An American Master.* New York: Scholastic Paperbacks, 2001.

Stewart, Mark. *Tiger Woods: Driving Force* (Sports Stars). Danbury, Conn.: Children's Press, 1998.

Woods, Earl, and Shari Wenk, with an introduction by Tiger Woods. *Start Something: You Can Make a Difference.* New York: Simon & Schuster, 2000.

INTERNET SITES

Club Tiger
http://www.clubtiger.com
The official site for the Tiger Woods fan club.

Golf Online
http://www.golfonline.com/
Biographies of various golfers plus news about the PGA tour.

Tiger Woods
http://www.tigerwoods.com/
Official site that includes biographical information, up-to-date news items, and details about the Tiger Woods Foundation.

Tiger Woods Foundation
http://www.twfound.org
For information about the Tiger Woods Foundation and its mission and goals.

Tiger Woods Timeline—Information Please Sports Almanac
http://www.infoplease.com/spot/ tigertime1.html
A timeline of Tiger Woods's life and accomplishments in the sport of golf.

Page numbers in *italics* indicate illustrations.

About the Author

Lucia Raatma received her bachelor's degree in English literature from the University of South Carolina and her master's degree in cinema studies from New York University. She has written a wide range of books for young people. When she is not researching or writing, she enjoys going to movies, playing tennis, practicing yoga, and spending time with her husband, daughter, and golden retriever. She lives in New York.